BUGS

ANTS

By William Anthony

KidHaven PUBLISHING

PHOTO CREDITS – Images are courtesy of Shutterstock.com. With thanks to Getty Images, Thinkstock Photo and iStockphoto.

Cover – Anna Molcharenko, Karramba Production, Ermak Oksana, ten43, azure1, Maciej Olszewski, desiger_an, Ortis, Manfred Ruckszio, Ohmega1982, Rapin_1981, schankz. Recurring Images – ten43, THPStock (paper), Ohmega1982 (header texture), Siarhei Dzmitryienkas (main background), designer_an (vector ants in header), Karramba Productions (parchment), Andrey Eremin, Steve Paint (labels), azure1 (magnifying glass), Ortis, enterphoto, oksana2010 (page decoration), Ermak Oksana (doodles). P1 – Anna Molcharenko, p2-3 – SweetCrisis, p4-5 – Ton Wang, NB Studio, Pavel Krasensky (web image), p6-7 – Sanimfocus, PI, p8-9 – kurt_G, Wladimir Lopes, p10-11 – kostasgr, Uros Medved, p12-13 – Pavel Krasensky, Mrs. Narawan Artayaku, p14-15 – Sergio Sallovitz, Dr Morley Read, p16-17 – frank60 (photo), p18-19 – Henrik Larsson, Tomatito, p20-21 – seamuss, oil-man, wan azizi, p22-23 – MvanCaspel, StockSmartStart, Mike McDonald, p24 – Anna Molcharenko

CONTENTS

Words that look like **THIS** can be found in the glossary on page 24.

EXPLORER TRAINING

You there – yes, you! Are you ready to become our new bug expert? Our team of explorers needs another member and you could be perfect for the job! However, first we need to train you.

This book will teach you all about ants. So grab your notepad and your magnifying glass, and get ready to get down in the dirt with these incredible insects!

WHAT IS AN ANT?

Before we start, we need to know about the different parts of an ant. Ants are a type of insect. Insects have no backbones and have six legs attached to their bodies.

The three main parts of an insect's body are the head, the thorax, and the abdomen.

Ants have two antennae attached to their heads. Ants use these to **SENSE** the world around them, as well as to tell other ants which nest they are from.

ADAPTATIONS

There are many different types of ants and they have all **ADAPTED** differently. Trap-jaw ants have tiny hairs on their jaws. If something brushes against these hairs, the ant's jaws slam shut.

Having fast jaws like these helps the trap-jaw ant to catch **PREY** that move very quickly.

Some ants have an adaptation that helps them to fly – wings. Some ants develop wings that let them fly away and leave their **COLONY** to start a new one.

Female ants lose their wings after they get older and **MATE.**

HOME LIFE

Ants have different types of homes. Some ants live underground, some live in mounds built on top of the ground, and others live in plants or trees.

Some ant nests are made up of tunnels and chambers, which are like rooms in a house. There can be tunnels in the ground where ants enter and exit the nest.

MEET THE COLONY

Every ant colony is made up of different ants that have different jobs. Colonies are normally made up of a queen ant, drones, workers, and alates. The queen ant is the leader of the colony.

Most ants you see outside the nest are worker ants.

Drones are males that mate with the queen ant. Worker ants are females that don't lay eggs. They build the nest and gather food. Alates have wings and leave the colony to start new ones elsewhere.

FINDING A FEAST

Worker ants find food for their colony. They leave the nest and return with food, usually during spring and summer. Each type of ant has a special set of jaws depending on what they use them for.

Leaf-cutter ants bite off sections of leaves and carry them back to the nest. They feed the leaves to a **FUNGUS**, which helps the fungus to grow. Then the ants eat the fungus.

BUILDING BRIDGES

Sometimes, it can be difficult to get food back home. Army ants work very well as a team. They do something special if there's a big gap that they can't jump over...

They build an ant bridge! Each ant hooks itself onto another to build a path for other ants to cross and move food over. Look – there's an ant bridge forming!

LIFE CYCLE

When the queen is ready to lay her eggs, it is the start of a new life cycle. In some **SPECIES** of ants, she will lay her eggs underground. During the day, the worker ants might move the eggs to warmer places.

The eggs eventually hatch into **LARVAE**, which have no eyes or legs and are shaped like worms. When the larvae are large enough, they change into pupae, which look much more like adult ants. Finally, the pupae become adults.

AMAZING ANTS

Ant colonies can be very big, but none are like the colony of Argentine ants in southern Europe. It starts in Italy, runs through France, and ends in Spain. That's 3,730 miles (6,000 km)!

Follow the black dots on the map to see where the colony runs.

The Argentine colony is made up of millions of nests, millions of queen ants, and billions of worker ants that are all able to work together.

TIME TO EXPLORE

Well, that's the end of your training. Good news – you've passed! You are now ready to go out and explore the wilderness, armed with your new knowledge. But there's one more thing you'll need before you go...

...your well-earned explorer's badge! Here it is, and it means you are now an ant expert. Why not make your own badge and wear it with pride? Congratulations, explorer!

GLOSSARY

adapt to change over time to suit the environment

colony a group of animals living in one place

fungus a living thing that often looks like a plant but has no flowers and lives on dead or decaying things

larvae types of young insects that must grow and change before they can reach their adult form

mate to produce young with an animal of the same species

prey animals that are hunted by other animals for food

sense to feel or be aware of

species a group of very similar animals or plants that are capable of producing more of their kind

INDEX